HERBERT HOWELLS

MINIATURES

FOR ORGAN

Kevin Mayhew

We hope you enjoy *Miniatures for Organ*.
Further copies of this and our many other books are available
from your local music shop or Christian bookshop.

In case of difficulty, please contact the publisher direct by writing to:

The Sales Department
KEVIN MAYHEW LTD
Rattlesden
Bury St Edmunds
Suffolk IP30 0SZ

Phone 01449 737978
Fax 01449 737834
E-mail info@kevinmayhewltd.com

Please ask for our complete catalogue of outstanding Church Music.

Acknowledgement
The 30 former sight-reading tests for piano by Herbert Howells contained
in this album were arranged by Alan Ridout for organ manuals only
with the permission of the Associated Board of the Royal Schools of Music
by which all rights are reserved.

Front Cover: *Gardeners* (1995) by Judy Byford (*b*.1965).
Courtesy of The Grand Design, Leeds/SuperStock Ltd, London.
Reproduced by kind permission.

Cover designed by Jaquetta Sergeant.

First published in Great Britain in 1993 by Kevin Mayhew Ltd.

ISBN 0 86209 391 0
Catalogue No: 3611053

1 2 3 4 5 6 7 8 9

Printed and bound in Great Britain by
Caligraving Limited Thetford Norfolk

Foreword

These pieces, recently rediscovered, were written in 1924 and 1937 by Herbert Howells as piano sight-reading tests for examinations of the Associated Board of the Royal Schools of Music. They are, however, much more than visual traps for the unwary. By turns graceful, surprising, and touching, they are inventive miniatures wholly characteristic of the composer; like the occasional pieces written for examination purposes by Ravel and Debussy they have a unique value. They have been slightly adapted here to make manuals only pieces for organ.

ONE

Herbert Howells (1892 - 1983)

TWO

Herbert Howells

THREE

Herbert Howells

FOUR

Herbert Howells

FIVE
Herbert Howells

SIX

Herbert Howells

SEVEN

Herbert Howells

EIGHT

Herbert Howells

NINE

Herbert Howells

TEN

Herbert Howells

ELEVEN

Herbert Howells

TWELVE

Herbert Howells

THIRTEEN

Herbert Howells

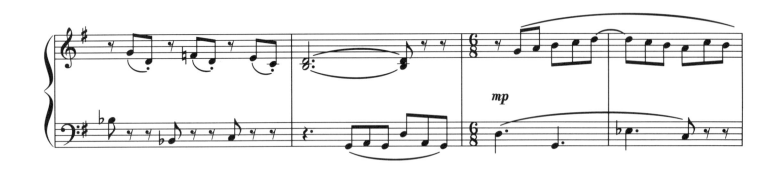

FOURTEEN

Herbert Howells

FIFTEEN

Herbert Howells

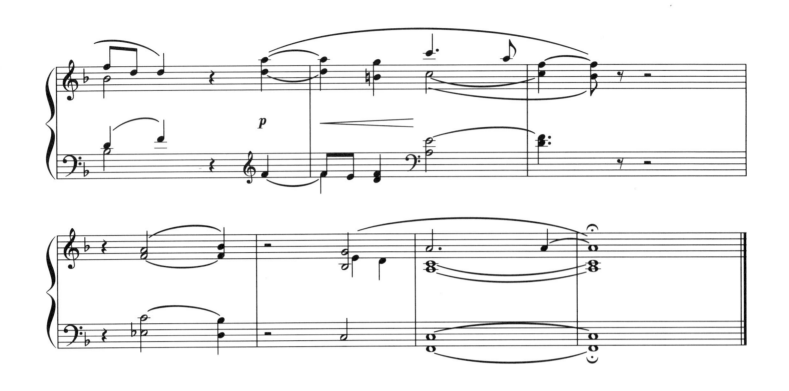

SIXTEEN

Herbert Howells

23

SEVENTEEN

Herbert Howells

Tempo di Gavotta

EIGHTEEN

Herbert Howells

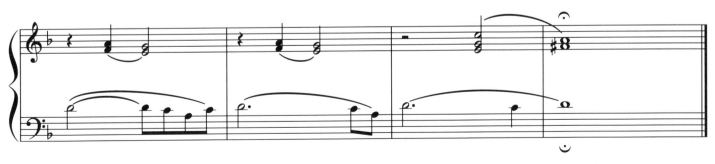

NINETEEN

Herbert Howells

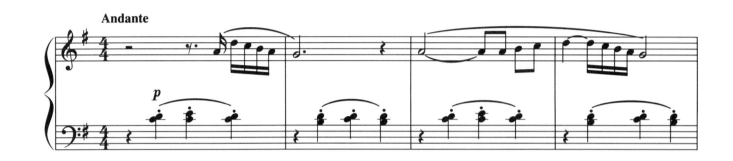

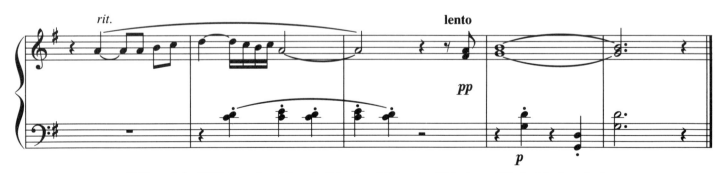

TWENTY

Herbert Howells

TWENTY ONE

Herbert Howells

TWENTY TWO

Herbert Howells

TWENTY THREE

Herbert Howells

TWENTY FOUR

Herbert Howells

TWENTY FIVE

Herbert Howells

TWENTY SIX
Herbert Howells

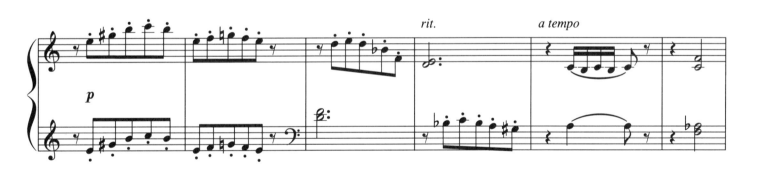

TWENTY SEVEN

Herbert Howells

TWENTY EIGHT

Herbert Howells

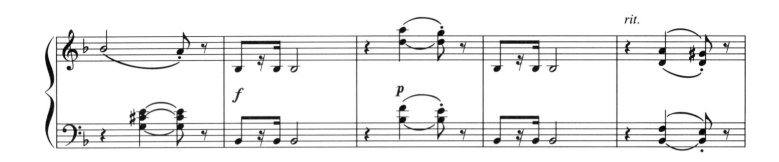

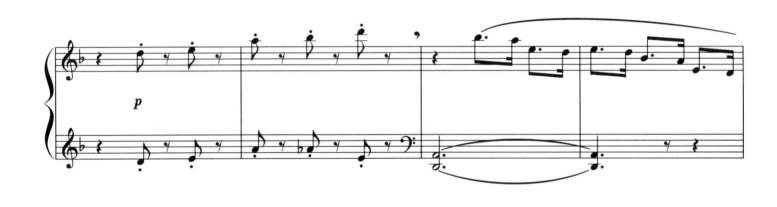

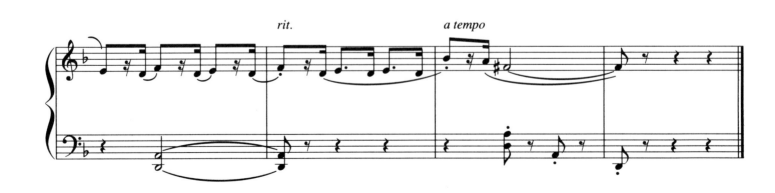

TWENTY NINE
Herbert Howells

THIRTY

Herbert Howells